A special gift for

_____

with love,

_____

date

_____

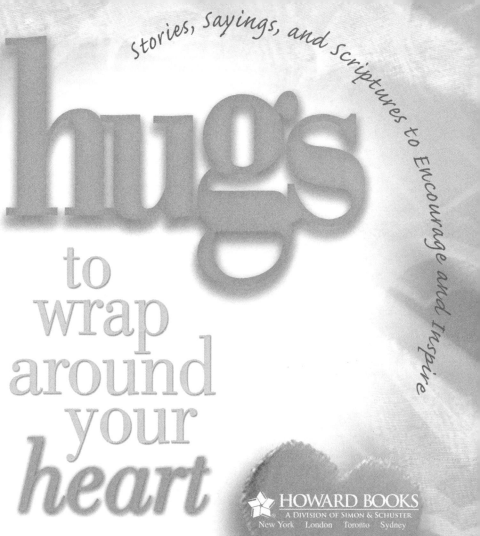

Stories, sayings, and scriptures to Encourage and Inspire

hug's
to wrap around your *heart*

HOWARD BOOKS
A DIVISION OF SIMON & SCHUSTER
New York London Toronto Sydney

10th Anniversary Limited Edition

Personalized Scriptures by
LeAnn Weiss

Our Purpose at Howard Books is to:

- *Increase faith* in the hearts of growing Christians
- *Inspire holiness* in the lives of believers
- *Instill hope* in the hearts of struggling people everywhere

Because He's coming again!

HOWARD
BOOKS

Published by Howard Books, a division of Simon & Schuster, Inc.
1230 Avenue of the Americas, New York, NY 10020
www.howardpublishing.com

Hugs to Wrap Around Your Heart © 2007 by Howard Books
Paraphrased scriptures © 2007 by LeAnnWeiss, 3006 Brandywine Drive,
Orlando, FL 32806; 407-898-4410

Library of Congress Cataloging-in-Publication Data
Weiss, LeAnn.
Hugs to wrap around your heart : personalized scriptures / by LeAnn Weiss.
—10 anniversary limited ed.
p. cm.
ISBN-13: 978-1-4165-5314-4
ISBN-10:   1-4165-5314-2
ISBN-13: 978-1-58229-715-6 (gift edition)
ISBN-10:   1-58229-715-0 (gift edition)
1. Spirituality. 2. Consolation. I. Title.
BV4501.3.W4225 2007
242—dc22
                                    2007015105

10 9 8 7 6 5 4 3 2 1

For information regarding special discounts for bulk purchases, please contact Simon &
Schuster Special Sales at 1-800-456-6798 or business@simonandschuster.com.

Edited by Chrys Howard
Cover design by Tennille Paden
Interior design by John Mark Luke Design
Photography from Photos.com

Contents

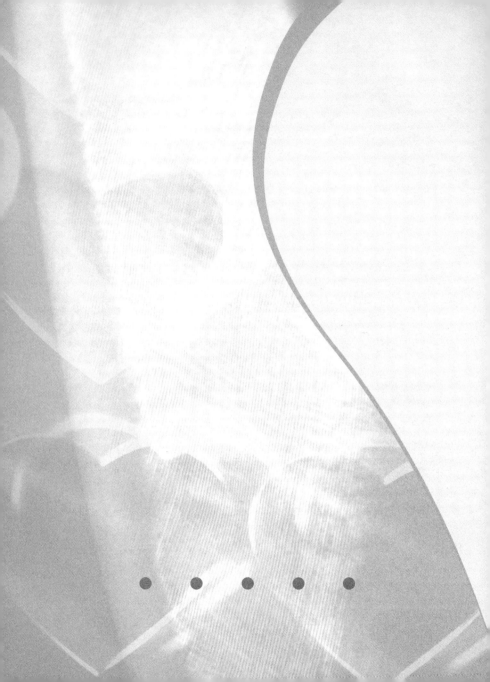

chapter 1

reaching

out

• • •

Every day I am your way, your truth, and your life. You can reach out because I strengthen you in all you do. And as you give, watch Me multiply blessings back to you in overflowing ways.

Generously,
Your God of Every Good and Perfect Gift

—FROM JOHN 14:6; PHILIPPIANS 4:13; LUKE 6:38; JAMES 1:17

We all feel at times like we're running on a hamster wheel. Just running, around and around, with no end in sight. Today, though, you jumped off! You left the dishes piled in the sink and ran to a friend who needed a shoulder to cry on. Or maybe you left work early, even though your desk was covered with paperwork, to buy Christmas presents for kids at the battered women and children's shelter down the road.

Whatever it was you did for someone else, it felt good. You traded all the tasks on your to-do list for something of greater significance.

And you noticed something. Nothing

dreadful happened. The earth kept spinning on its axis. No natural disasters could be traced back to your change in schedule.

In fact, sometimes it's exactly when life seems to be spinning out of control—when you just don't think you could possibly help anybody else because your life is such a mess—that we need to reach out. Somehow you just do it, and afterward you know why it pays to go the extra mile.

Who knows, maybe you really needed that walk more than the person who asked you to join her. At any rate, it sure beats running on that wheel.

I have *learned* that what we have done for ourselves alone dies with us. What we have done for others and the world *remains* and is immortal.

• • •

Albert Pike

The Gift

The phone rang as Cheryl was starting another load of laundry. It was the third one she'd done that day, along with cleaning the bathrooms, vacuuming the entire house, mopping the kitchen floor, and taking care of the three children—all while her husband sat in his home office leisurely working at the computer. Cheryl had thought Gary's going into business for himself and having his office at home would be great for the family. But now she realized that meant her husband never left work. Working was all he seemed to be doing these days.

"I'm not answering!" Cheryl hollered to Gary. "I don't have time to talk to anyone." She knew she sounded haggard. That was how she felt, and she wanted Gary to know it. Today was Saturday. She'd been trying to make her feelings known all week.

Ring, ring. "This is the Stone residence. Sorry we missed your call . . ." Cheryl could hear the answering machine from the hall. *Figures*, she thought. *Gary can't even take the time to answer the phone around here.* Then she muttered under her breath to whoever might be calling. "Don't hold your breath. 'As soon as possible' is gonna be a while."

Gary had decided to quit his job to become an independent contractor three months earlier with Cheryl's full support. He had plenty of computer expertise, and they felt confident he could get enough consulting work to make a good living. She just hadn't realized how hard he would have to work to make that happen.

For all her grumpiness, Cheryl knew Gary was a good husband. He'd always participated fully with the three children, waking up for nighttime feedings when they were babies, taking turns shuttling the oldest to school and practice for whatever sport was in season. He'd stop by the grocery store or the pizza place on the way home from work to pick up supper, and he'd throw in a load or two of laundry when necessary. They had been a good team—always busy, but somehow it had worked. Until recently.

Cheryl understood that Gary was feeling the burden of responsibility to make it in his new venture and be able to support the family. *This is only for a little while, until he gets going,* she kept telling herself. But lately the positive self-talk was being drowned out by self-pity. *Sure, he's working, but I work full-time too, plus I'm doing everything else around here.* Their second-grader had homework at least a couple of nights a week, and the twin toddlers were a handful—the house seemed in a continual state of disaster. Cheryl was worn out and at the end of her rope. And when Gary didn't answer the phone, it felt like the last straw.

Her mental grumbling was interrupted by the voice on the answering machine. "Cheryl, this is Laura. I was hoping we could do something fun together this evening. I really need a break from the hospital and could use someone to talk to."

Cheryl immediately felt awful. That was her best friend in the entire world. Laura's father had had a stroke on

Monday. The doctors didn't think he would ever fully recover. Cheryl had gone to the hospital when it happened
but had been so busy since then that she'd hardly even
checked on Laura, except for one measly call to ask how
her dad was doing.

I have to call her back, she thought, *but there's no way
I can go.* There was more laundry to do, bills to pay, and
groceries to shop for. Besides, who would watch the kids?
If she left them home while Gary was working, they'd just
destroy the house she'd worked all day to clean. She'd
never get all the chores done before the new week started
and they piled up all over again. She picked up the phone
to somehow gracefully decline the invitation.

"When are you leaving?" Gary hollered.

"What do you mean, when am I leaving?" she retorted,
not bothering to disguise her aggravation.

"I mean, I think you should go," Gary said with a smile
as he joined her in the kitchen. "I'll stay home with the
kids and keep the laundry going and do whatever else was
on your list for the day."

"But what about your work?"

The Gift

"It can wait. Your friend is more important. Besides, you need a little fun in your life too."

I couldn't agree more! she thought. "I don't know what's gotten into you, but I'll take you up on that offer!" Cheryl hugged her husband and happily picked up the phone to dial her best friend before he had a chance to change his mind.

After a quick conversation and a plan for Cheryl to pick up Laura at the hospital so they could ride together and talk on the way to the restaurant, Cheryl threw on some lipstick, slipped on her boots, kissed the kids good-bye, and was out the door. She turned around quickly though, poked her head back inside, and yelled, "Don't forget to give the kids baths so they're clean for church in the morning." Her step was feeling a little lighter, but the knot in her stomach that had grown and tightened over the past few months was still there.

When she arrived at the hospital, Cheryl was struck by what a difficult thing Laura must be going through. She was an only child, and she had lost her mother just two years before. Somehow, though, Cheryl couldn't quite stop her mind from drifting back to her own problems.

"Thanks so much for rescuing me," Laura said as she met her friend at the front desk. "I can't tell you how much I needed this."

"Well, I have to admit, my life has been crazy lately, and getting away seemed almost too monumental a task when I first heard your message." Then, guiltily, "But I always have time for you."

As the two friends walked through the parking garage, the conversation kept going back to Cheryl and how stressful her situation was. She knew she should be letting her friend vent instead of complaining. But she couldn't stop worrying about whether her husband was really doing what he said he would or if he had slipped back to his office. She was going to lose it if she came home to a houseful of chores and dirty children.

As they approached the car, she noticed Laura looking in the window of an old brown Chevy Caprice that had definitely seen better days. Cheryl muttered an attempt at humor, "I think they need to haul that clunker off to the junkyard."

But Laura didn't laugh. She started rummaging in her

overcrowded purse. Cheryl saw her friend pull out a paper from her wallet and lean into the open window of the "clunker."

"Oh!" Cheryl stuttered. "I—I hope I didn't offend you by making fun of that car. Were you leaving a note for someone you know?"

"No," Laura replied somewhat mysteriously. "Come on; let's go enjoy a wonderful meal. I'm sick of hospital food."

But Cheryl's curiosity was aroused. She came around to where Laura was standing and peeked into the window of the old car. A bright yellow notice with a red FINAL stamp on it was lying face-up on the seat. It was an electric bill for $98.99. Then something else caught her eye. Tucked under that notice, just barely showing, was the corner of what looked like money.

Cheryl knew instantly what Laura had done. Her friend had always been kind-hearted, but seeing her do something that generous in the midst of such a difficult time in her life brought tears to Cheryl's eyes. *What a contrast to my wallowing in self-pity*, she thought, ashamed. Today, while she'd been busy thinking only of herself, her husband had set aside what he was doing and thought of her. And her friend, who was in the midst of her own turmoil, had listened to Cheryl's little grievances and helped someone she didn't even know. It was a living illustration of how to set aside her problems and think of someone else.

She turned and hugged Laura as tightly as she could. "Thanks, Laura."

"For what? I didn't give you the money," Laura joked.

"For reminding me how truly blessed I am."

from *Hugs to Brighten Your Day*
by Ashley Moore & Korie Robertson

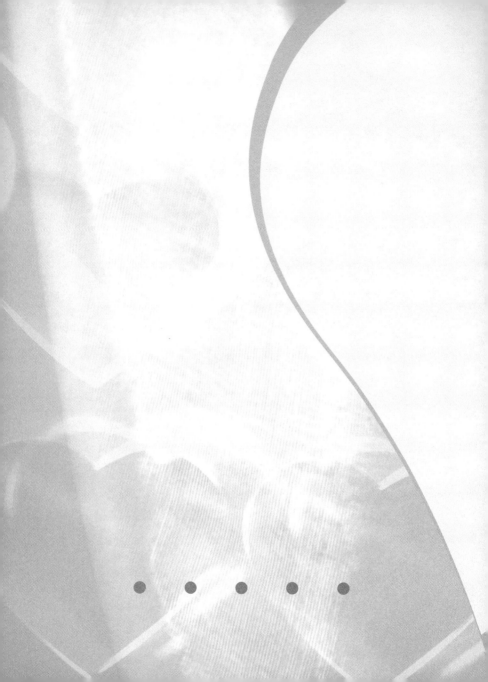

chapter 2

a sister's
perspective

• • • •

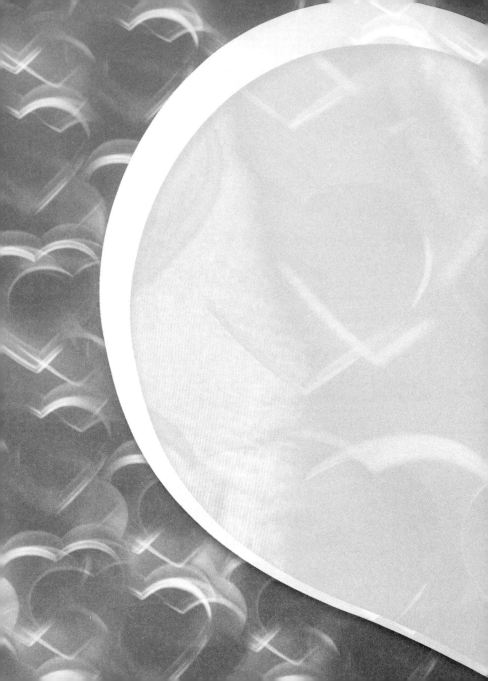

Let your soul be at rest once more.

I've been good to you . . .

delivering your soul from death

and your eyes from tears.

May you walk before Me in the

land of the living. My supernatural peace,

which transcends all

human understanding, will guard your

heart and your mind.

Peacefully,
Your Father of Life

—FROM PSALM 116:7–9; PHILIPPIANS 4:7

Sisters. There's something about the bond of sisterhood that is unlike all other unions. There's the shared femaleness—that alone is significant, but there's so much more. There's the unreasoning bond of heritage—you're bound together just because of who you are. And there's the unrelenting bond of shared experiences—you've shared secrets and Barbie dolls, Christmas mornings and roller skates. And then there's the inexplicable bond of shared genes and genetic codes that make it so much fun to say, "You look just like Mama Lou when you say that!" or "Your lasagna tastes exactly like Mom's!"

But this bond, this sameness, has a strange way of bringing our differences into sharp focus. And sometimes we can learn qualities or perspectives from our sisters that we do not naturally possess.

Take Mary and Martha, for instance. When Jesus came to their home, each approached her honored guest through her own distinct personality. Martha, the gracious hostess, took her responsibilities very seriously. She cooked and cleaned and fussed and fixed.

Mary, on the other hand, took Jesus seriously. Everything else could wait. All other responsibilities were put on hold. The Lord was in their house, and she wanted to hear every word He had to say.

On that day, Martha learned from Mary that, really, "only one thing is needed" (Luke 10:42). On another day, Mary may have learned from Martha the value of a job well done.

Sisterhood provides a safe place to learn new ideas, to explore different ways of looking at life. The comfort of our sameness helps us relax enough to learn from our differences.

So get comfortable. Put your feet up. Spend some time reflecting on the blessings of being a sister. You'll be glad you did.

When all the dust is settled and
all the crowds are *gone,*
the things that matter are
faith, family, and friends.

• • •

Barbara Bush

Peace Like a River

She didn't know why they had come. But here they stood, under the trees. Three sisters, side by side, arms around one another's waists. They were here to visit their brother's grave.

It had been a little more than three years since Paul had died, but when people asked Michele, the oldest of the three sisters, about her siblings, she still spoke of Paul in the present: "I have three brothers and two sisters," she'd say. She firmly believed that Paul was still very much alive—just not here.

When her sister Katherine had suggested they visit Paul's grave, Michele had hesitated. She always had a hard time understanding why people went to visit graves—especially people of faith who believed that their loved ones were with God. The person was not there. Why attach such sentiment to a grave?

"Come on, Michele," the youngest sister, Mattilyn, had coaxed, "just come so we can be together."

Michele had reluctantly agreed to go.

She loved being with her sisters. She always felt an unexplainable joy and sense of completion just being with them. No three women could be more different. Mattilyn had the air of a businesswoman—always organizing, always planning. She gave financial advice to all her siblings and even took care of the accounting for their father's business. Katherine was the maternal homemaker. Baking bread, going to yard sales, and refinishing furniture were some of her favorite pastimes. Easygoing and completely candid, she liked nothing more than long conversations of honest sharing. Michele's demeanor was somewhere between Mattilyn's efficiency and Katherine's candor. She loved learning and being outdoors and spent way too many hours indoors at work. But the bond between them did not require common interests or similar personalities. Their bond was based on a shared heritage and a sense of family. Their love was rooted in who they were: they were sisters.

Their busy chatter on the way to the cemetery had jumped from their relationships with their husbands to their children's activities, to the demands of work, to experiences at church. It was wonderful to share the day-to-day aspects of their lives in an atmosphere of complete trust and love.

When they arrived at the cemetery, Mattilyn knew just where the grave site was. As they walked among other tombstones on the way to their brother's, their mood quieted. And now the three of them stood together, sharing unspoken feelings, uniting their spirits.

Michele remembered the morning she got the call and the heaviness in her mother's voice. "Paul's had a heart attack," her mother said. "He died before he got to the hospital."

Michele had sat in a stupor on the side of the bed, eyes staring straight ahead, mouth hanging open, receiver dangling in her hand. Her hurriedly thrown-on robe was still unbuttoned. Tears streamed down her face. She just sat. No thoughts formed. No emotions took shape. She was aware only of the pain.

She remembered standing in front of Paul's open coffin at the funeral home with her two sisters—in the same pose they now maintained. Loud sobs had threatened to spill from her mouth. Instead, the three women cried quietly together. The song the congregation sang at the church memorial service the previous night played in her head: "When peace like a river attendeth my way, when sorrows like sea billows roll; whatever my lot, Thou hast taught me to say, 'It is well, it is well with my soul.'" It had been her brother's favorite song. He even rewrote the words into simple, contemporary language, and a copy of his rendition hung on Michele's den wall. As she looked down upon his stiff, cold body, she realized that her brother's death brought her family's faith into sharp focus: *So this is what my faith is all about*, she thought. *If I believe what I've professed to believe all my life, then I know that Paul will be raised someday, and we'll all be with him again. If that isn't true, then none of what I believe is true.* But Michele knew that it was.

And now they stood together at his grave, the truth

of his absence made fresh again. And with the truth, the pain.

"Remember the time . . ." Mattilyn began, and for the next several minutes they shared stories of their childhood and growing up together. They laughed a little, cried some, then fell silent as each rummaged through her own treasure box of memories.

The hot sun filtered through the summer green leaves above them. A gentle breeze mercifully cooled their faces. The only sounds heard were the cars on the distant freeway. Each woman was absorbed in her own thoughts. Sadness began to clutch at Michele's heart. She wished they had not come. This place made her think only of death and separation. She was about to insist they leave when a scratchy song rose up through the silence.

"When peace like a river . . ."

Michele was roused from her brooding.

" . . . attendeth my way," the voice continued.

It was Katherine. She was singing Paul's song. Her voice was weak and filled with tears, but she sang on.

"When sorrows like sea billows roll . . ." Mattilyn joined in.

a sister's *perspective*

Michele heard her own voice join the others, and all three sang haltingly in unison, "Whatever my lot, Thou hast taught me to say, 'It is well, it is well with my soul.'"

At that moment, no force could have pulled the three sisters apart. Clinging to each other for support, their voices gained strength as they sang on, "And, Lord, haste the day when my faith shall be sight, the clouds be rolled back as a scroll, the trump shall resound, and the Lord shall descend, even so, it is well with my soul."

As their song concluded, a vague understanding began to come over Michele. At first she didn't recognize what it was. But her emotions took form, and she began to understand why it was good they had come. They had come to share memories of someone they loved; they had come to be reminded of their eternal hope. They had come to honor their brother Paul. Not because they thought that in some sense he was still there, but because they knew Whose he was and where he was. Maybe he was even looking down on them right now. Maybe he was even singing with them.

She closed her eyes and could see his face. She saw the mischievous twinkle in his eyes and his easy, gentle smile. She heard his sweet voice. And with the memory came a wonderful sensation. She felt it go all through her. Slow . . . cool . . . calm. She took a deep breath, and the feeling intensified—refreshing her tired heart, soothing her soul. It flooded her body, almost in a physical sense, and filled her with an all-consuming sense of well-being. Then she knew what it was. It was peace—the peace that Paul had loved to sing about—the peace that must accompany him now. Peace.

Peace . . . like a river.

She was glad they had come.

from *Hugs for Sisters*
by Philis Boultinghouse

chapter 3

sweet

motivation

• • •

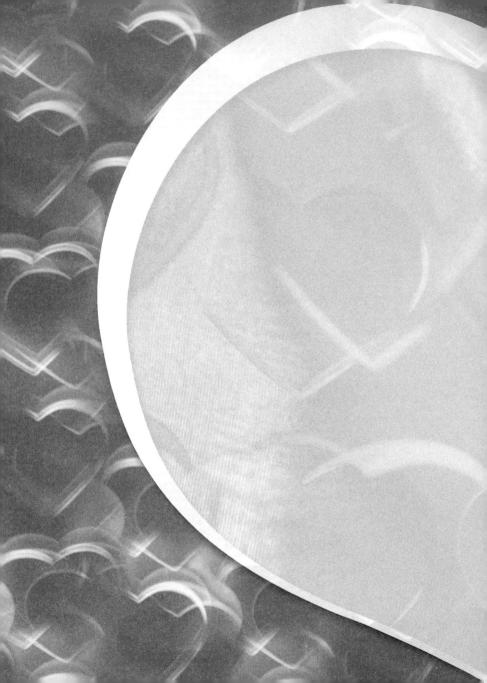

Desiring good things will lead to
sweet satisfaction. May you spur
each other on to love and
good deeds. Taste and experience
My absolute goodness, and know
that My goodness and love will surround you
each and every day.

Thinking sweet thoughts of you,
Your God of Light

—FROM PROVERBS 13:25; HEBREWS 10:24;
    PSALMS 34:8; 23:6

One of the greatest sacrifices dieters face is giving up chocolate. Chocolate is high in calories and saturated fat, so no matter how much they adore it, some try to give it up.

But listen up, chocolate lovers: there are many legitimate reasons to make chocolate a part of your healthy, balanced diet. Dark chocolate reduces high blood pressure, protects blood vessels, promotes heart health, and helps prevent some cancers. Plus, chocolate wakes us up and gets us moving. Chocolate lovers know the physical and emotional lift that comes from eating it. Caffeine and other stimulants in chocolate increase the activity of neurotransmitters in the brain, making it easier to pay attention and stay alert.

But perhaps chocolate's best aid to dieters is sweet motivation. As a reward for careful eating, nothing beats chocolate's power to modify behavior. Who can't be good all day when she knows there's chocolate ice cream for dessert? Who wouldn't work out a little longer at the gym in exchange for a square of the rich stuff?

When we desire good things—like chocolate, an education, a strong relationship, or self-improvement— we're much more likely to work hard to achieve them. Working toward good goals and achieving them is sure to bring great satisfaction. What do you desire? How will you reach your goals? With hard work and determination—and maybe a little chocolate motivation— you can do it!

A true *chocolate* lover
finds ways to accommodate
his *passion* and make it
work with his lifestyle.

. . .

Julie Davis

One Sweet Diet

It was a mystery—a mystery that was practically driving Emmy Bond crazy. Or maybe it was just hunger.

"Where's Trixie?" Emmy's oldest sister, Donna, quizzed her about their middle sister as Emmy slid into the restaurant booth across from her.

"I don't know," Emmy replied, trying to hide her curiosity about the whole situation. "I didn't see her car in the parking lot."

"It's not like her to be late," Donna said, stirring Sweet'n Low into her iced tea with a fat red straw. "Why didn't she pick you up like she usually does?"

"Who knows?" Emmy shrugged, pulling her purse off her shoulder and stowing it on the seat beside her. "She called yesterday and told me to drive myself. Left a message on my machine saying she'd just meet us here—again.

Something's up with that girl." Emmy leaned conspiratorially across the table. "Do you think something's wrong, Donna? Change of life, maybe?"

"Shh," Donna hissed. Her eyes sent a warning Emmy understood instantly.

"You're late." Donna slid over to make room on the seat for Trixie to sit beside her.

"I was here on time." Trixie dismissed the accusation with a wave of her hand as she sat down. "I was in the restroom freshening up a little."

Emmy searched Donna's eyes for some reaction. Neither said anything. They looked away as the waiter came to take Emmy and Trixie's drink orders.

"A Mountain Dew sure is tempting," Emmy said ruefully. She patted her stomach, then closed her menu with resolve. "But I'll be good. Especially with these two watching." She nodded at her sisters. "I'll just have water."

"I'll have the same, and I think we're ready to order." Trixie looked to Donna and Emmy for confirmation.

Emmy could have told the waiter what Donna would order: a half-sized grilled chicken salad with fat-free ranch dressing—on the side, no breadstick. But Emmy was starving. She wanted the twelve-ounce sirloin with sautéed mushrooms, Cheddar potatoes, and garlic bread. But since the sisters' diet pact, she had made it a rule never to order anything that weighed more ounces than the pants size she was trying to fit into—eight.

Who was she kidding? Right now she'd be happy just to fit into a size twelve. She sighed in resignation and ordered the vegetable plate—hold the cheese sauce. With great interest, Emmy waited to hear what Trixie would order.

"I'll take the grilled tilapia with mango salsa and a side of rice," Trixie said, sliding the menu back to the waiter. "And then I'd like the hot-fudge chocolate-brownie cake for dessert." She smiled at the stick-thin young waiter, who nodded and left to place their order. "He's kind of cute," she remarked offhandedly. "But he could use a few more pounds."

"And a few more years," Donna added.

"I'd be more than happy to donate a few of mine," Emmy volunteered. "Pounds *and* years."

Donna turned suddenly toward Trixie. "So you're really serious about this?"

"About the waiter?" Trixie asked innocently. "He's just a little eye candy."

"Not the waiter," Donna waved her off impatiently. "You're serious about this . . . this chocolate *diet* of yours?"

"I'm serious all right," Trixie replied, smoothing her shirt over her waist. "It satisfies the sweet tooth without offending the stomach. What's more, it's really working. I'm down another four pounds, and I have way more energy than I used to."

Emmy eyed Trixie carefully. She had to admit that her sister did look thinner. She could see it clearly in her face: there was more definition in her cheeks and jawline. She was pretty sure her sister's sporty warm-up suit was new as well, a good indication that Trixie had dropped another size. *But there's no such thing as a chocolate diet! How is she doing it?*

"I refuse to believe a chocolate diet can work." Donna was clearly exasperated. "It's counterintuitive. That dessert you ordered must have seven hundred calories. You can't lose weight with a diet that allows for that every day. It's just not possible!"

Trixie's eyes danced mischievously. "If it's not possible, how do you explain my losing twenty-five pounds in just over two months?"

"I don't know," Donna admitted, looking miserable. "I can't. All I know is that I've been religiously counting calories and cutting out fat. I haven't had even a taste of chocolate in months—yet I've only lost nine and a half pounds."

"And your sense of humor," Emmy teased. "Relax, Donna, it's nothing personal. We're both a little grumpy since we started dieting. You have to admit your calorie counting makes you a little uptight. I never see you without your little calorie book. I, on the other hand, dream constantly about carbs—pasta, bread, mashed potatoes, French fries, ice cream . . . hot-fudge chocolate-brownie cake . . ." Her words trailed off as she imagined the taste and texture of her forbidden tempters.

"You're the one who chose low carb," Donna scolded. "You thought it would be easier than the sensible low-fat, low-cal diet I chose."

"It seemed pretty sensible compared to Trixie's chocolate diet," Emmy said, defending her decision. "Who ever heard of a diet that lets you eat chocolate? Are you really eating chocolate every day, Trix?"

"I swear." Trixie raised her hand as if taking an oath.

"And you're not starving yourself the rest of the day?" Emmy probed.

"I haven't missed a single meal."

"Are you being careful to eat a balanced diet?" Donna pushed. "Getting enough dairy, fiber, fruits, and veggies?"

"Oh yes," Trixie promised.

The conversation halted as the waiter brought their food. He accidentally placed Trixie's fish in front of Emmy, and she fought a sudden urge to grab the garlic toast. But Trixie seemed to read her mind and quickly exchanged plates.

Emmy didn't even close her eyes or hear the short prayer Trixie said before they ate; she stared hungrily at that bread.

"So what's your secret?" Emmy asked, her eyes following the bread as Trixie raised it to her mouth and took a bite. "How can you eat chocolate every day and still lose weight so easily when it's such a struggle for Donna and me?"

"Losing weight isn't easy for anyone," Trixie admitted. "But think about the psychology of eating. It's as emotional as it is physical. Diets never work if you end up feeling deprived."

"*I* feel deprived," Emmy admitted, grabbing Trixie's bread as soon as she put it down.

"That's why people fall off the wagon." Trixie stared meaningfully at Emmy, whose mouth was full of Trixie's toast.

"Hey, it's bread." Emmy defended herself, a dry crumb shooting indecorously across the table. "It has to be better for me than chocolate!"

Trixie's smile looked genuinely sympathetic. "If we can unravel the mystery of the psychology of dieting, we have a better chance of success."

"Sounds like mumbo jumbo to me," Donna said sullenly, savagely attacking the dry leaves of her salad.

Trixie ignored her. "Chocolate is how I reward myself for being good. And because I love chocolate so much, I'm *very* motivated to be good."

"But hot-fudge chocolate-brownie cake just has to outweigh any good you can be gaining from doing well on your diet," Emmy insisted, polishing off the last of her steamed broccoli.

"Ah, but you can't overlook the importance of exercise," Trixie said.

"Well, that explains the athletic clothes." Emmy ran her finger across her plate, trying to get every last drop of butter sauce. "You joined a gym!" Trixie shook her head. "Hired a personal trainer?"

"No! I've just been walking more—and drinking more water too." Trixie raised her glass for a refill as a waiter walked by with a pitcher. "Both will speed up your metabolism. Burning more calories means you can eat more."

"But still . . . ," Donna protested. "I just can't believe it. I mean, come on, it's chocolate!"

As if on cue, Trixie's dessert arrived. No one spoke, but all eyes lingered enviously on the luscious-looking treat as Trixie slowly savored every bite.

Emmy realized she was unconsciously licking her lips. *This is torture. I can't watch this.* She stood up abruptly, picked up the check, and headed toward the cashier. "My treat today. Meet me at the door when you're done."

Donna and Trixie joined her a few minutes later, and

she followed them outside. Yes, she could tell that both her sisters had lost weight, but Trixie really looked fantastic. Maybe she should quit skipping carbs and start eating chocolate too. That would be one sweet diet.

Outside, Donna turned left and Emmy went the opposite direction.

"I'm parked over here," Donna said.

"I'm this way." Emmy turned to Trixie, who was fumbling in her purse. "Which way are you?"

"I'm going your way."

"Bye, then," Donna said. "You'd better have parked really far away if you're hoping to walk off that chocolate, Trix."

"Oh, I did." Trixie laughed. She and Emmy waved at Donna and headed the other direction.

"Here's my car." Emmy opened her car door.

"See you later, little sis." Trixie put her hand warmly on Emmy's shoulder. "Thanks for lunch."

"You're welcome." Emmy put on her most powerful little-sister pouty face. "You know, you're setting the bar on this diet so high that I'll never be able to live up to your example. You're supposed to help your younger sister succeed, not make her decide it's not even worth trying."

"Is that how you feel?" Trixie seemed surprised.

Emmy nodded piteously, milking the pressure for all it was worth. "Don't you think you should let me in on your secret—and help me learn how to lose weight like you're doing?"

"Seriously, Em. It's all in the walking. I'd be happy to walk with you if you're serious. If you want, I can swing by your place tomorrow, and we can walk together. Would you like that?"

"I sure would!" Emmy beamed. *This is going to be great!* "See you tomorrow." Emmy climbed into her car, then stopped and shouted toward Trixie, who was moving away. "Uh, Trix, where *is* your car?" Emmy asked, curiously.

Trixie's eyes twinkled. "At home, in my garage."

"What?" Emmy gasped, realization slowly dawning. "But that has to be five miles away!"

"If you cut across the park, it's four point two," Trixie corrected, checking something in her hand—a pedometer—which she hooked on her waistband. "And four point two miles home again. More than enough to make up for hot-fudge chocolate-brownie cake. And if I had known you were paying, I would have gotten it with ice cream!" She laughed. "But don't tell Donna yet, OK? It's kind of fun driving her nuts." And with a wink, Trixie sauntered away.

from *Hugs for Chocolate Lovers*
by Tammy L. Bicket and Dawn M. Brandon

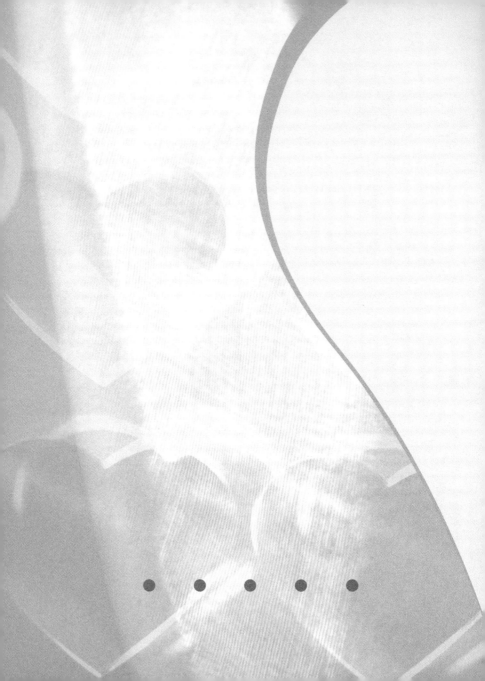

shaping
minds

• • •

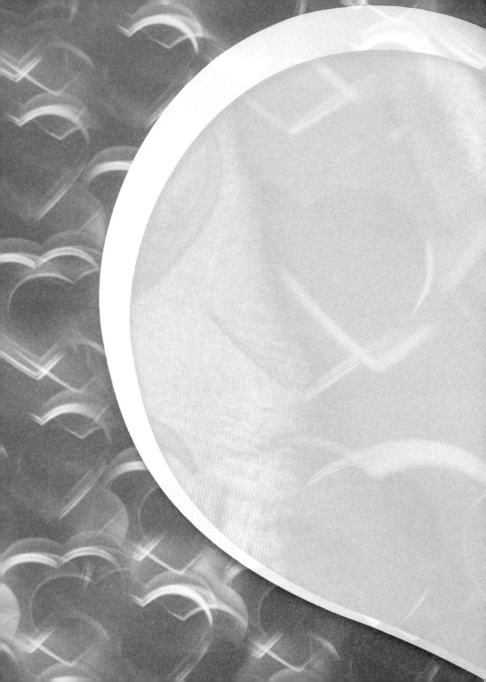

Your teachings have great importance!
What you teach guides your
children when they walk and watches
over them while they sleep. Your
instructions are lights for their
lives and speak to them even when
you aren't there.

Love,
Your God of Wisdom

—Proverbs 6:20–23

You may not have a professional degree, but you are a world-class teacher all the same. And you practice your profession on a daily basis—not on a college campus or behind a podium in a marble-floored classroom—but right there in the warmth of your carefully kept home.

While you've gone about the rigorous routines of motherhood, little eyes have watched and little minds and hearts have been shaped for eternity. Your young pupils have learned of sacrificial love as they've seen you take the last and least so others can have more. They've learned to distinguish right from wrong as they've observed your life of honesty and integrity. They've learned about faith as they've heard you pray to an unseen God—sometimes in tears, sometimes with thanksgiving, always with a firm belief that God is real, that he hears your prayers, and that he responds faithfully. They've learned that failure is not final as they've seen you confess your own faults and offer generous forgiveness to others. Above all they've learned what real love means— it means sharing hurts, hopes, joys, and homecomings; it means staying when it would be easier to leave, defending when others accuse, holding on when you're tempted to let go, and letting go when you desperately want to hold on. The same lips that have countless times formed the word "Mom," will say, "Thanks, Mom, for your precious teachings. You're the best."

My *mother* was the most
beautiful woman I ever saw.
All I am I *owe* to my mother.
I attribute all my success in
life to the *moral,* intellectual
and physical education
I received from *her.*

• • •

George Washington

Learning to Read

My mother taught me to read. She didn't mean to—I mean she wasn't trying to—but she did. I do not know when she began the practice, but I do know that, from my earliest remembrances, she read to me every day before my nap—except Saturday and Sunday. On weekdays, my father was at work and my sister at school, so we would crawl into my parents' bed and prop the pillows up against the iron post of the bedstead—after fluffing them up, of course. What a shame that modern children don't even know the word *fluffing*. They don't know it because they don't fluff—you can't fluff polyester and foam rubber. We've added *microchip* to our vocabulary and deleted *fluffing*. It was a sorry exchange, and our language is the more barren for it. Anyway, we would fluff the pillows, nestle back into them, and huddle very close to each other, and she would read.

shaping *minds*

What did she read? The Bible of course—what else? It was the only book in our house. She read stories from the Bible.

She was a finger reader.

When I first read at school, I read the same way; but my teacher, Miss Smokey, absolutely forbade it. I told her my mother read that way, and she said it was okay for my mother but not for me. Miss Smokey was very nice—and she meant well—but I'm really glad that my mother's teacher didn't forbid her to read with her finger because if she had, you see, I wouldn't have learned nearly so soon or so well, and I might not have loved it so.

Oh, you may not know what finger reading is. It's like fluffing, I guess. Finger reading is following the words with your finger so you won't lose your place or jump to the wrong line. It makes perfectly good sense if you think about it. In schools nowadays, we're very concerned with how fast people read. If you can read a thousand words a minute, that is absolutely fantastic—and it really doesn't matter if you understand the words or enjoy them or take the time to think about them. You must learn to read them

Learning to Read

very quickly—because there are so many of them—and if you don't read them quickly, my goodness, you may never read all of them. And reading all of them is terribly important, even though most of them aren't worth much.

My mother was a finger reader. Every day as she read, I would hear her voice and watch her finger as it went back and forth across the page. Of course it happened very slowly—and I didn't *know* I was learning to read. I honestly didn't even mean to learn—it was quite an *accident*. I began to associate what my mother was saying with the word above her finger. There were lots of *ands*, *thats*, and *buts*, and I guess I learned those first. It was easy for an uncluttered mind to grasp that it took a long time to say *Belshazzar* and that it also took a lot of letters. The more I learned, the more fascinated I became with my mother's voice and her moving finger.

One day I corrected her. She either mispronounced or skipped a word—I don't remember which—and I corrected her. She was incredulous. "How did you know that?" she asked. I didn't know how I knew. I just knew that the word she said wasn't the word that was above her finger. I did not know the alphabet—that would come much later in

shaping *minds*

school. I didn't know phonics—I still don't—but I could tell a telephone pole from a fire hydrant, and I could tell the difference between Jehu and Jerusalem. My mother asked me to read, and I did it gladly—slowly, haltingly—finger under the words. With her coaching, I read. Then I read with no coaching, and we took turns. Mom read one day—I read the next.

When I went to school a couple of years later, Miss Smokey tried to teach me to read. I told her I could already read. I could tell it hurt her feelings, so I said I was sorry—but reading was a piece of cake. They were reading Dick and Jane, and I knew Nebuchadnezzar, Jebusite, Perrizzite, Shamgar, and Rehoboam. I told her she could teach me math—

I was real dumb in that.

But I want you to see—that if my mother was teaching me to read—without meaning to—she was also teaching me about God, about right and wrong, about good and evil. Yes, those ideas were forming in my mind—waiting for the moment when I would need them to help me understand my growing, changing world.

Learning to Read

She didn't mean to—any more than she meant to teach me to read. She read the Bible because she loved to read the Bible—because it had great meaning to her. If I hadn't been around, she would have read it anyway; and after I went to school and didn't take naps anymore, she continued to read. She only knew that it entertained me and that it was good for me in some general way.

Again, my specific point is that both teaching me to read and teaching me about God—about good and evil and standing for the right—did not come to me through lectures and sermons, although I heard plenty of them at church; they came to me through my mother's attempt to establish and strengthen her own relationship with God.

Her daily awareness of his providence,
Her constant devotion to his will,
her love for his word—
passed to me—naturally.

from *Hugs for Mom*
by John William Smith

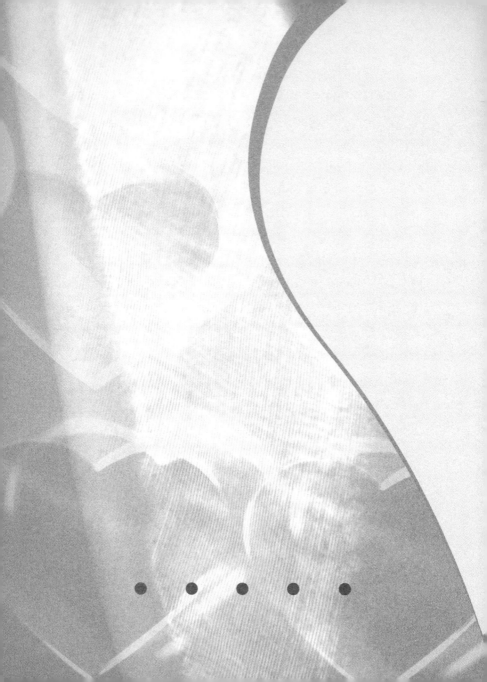

chapter 5

you have a secret—
share it

• • •

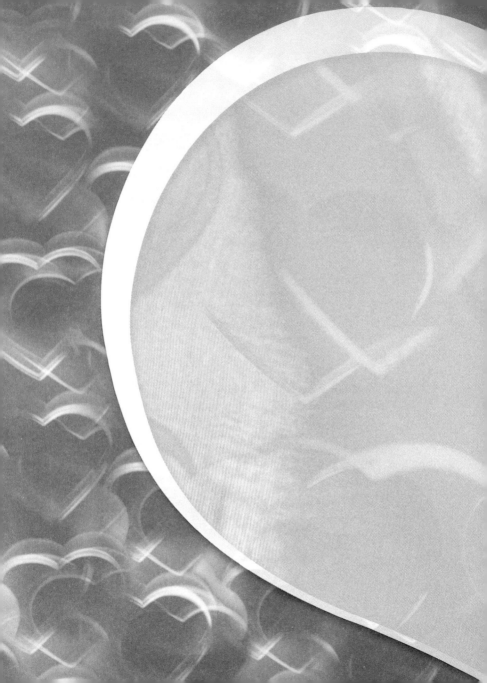

I've searched you and know you. The secret things in life belong to Me! But the treasures I've revealed to you belong to you and your family to be passed down for generations. And be patient—I'm not finished with you yet! I'm still in the process of completing the good work I started in you.

Intimately,

Your Creator and God

—FROM PSALM 139:1; DEUTERONOMY 29:29; PHILIPPIANS 1:6

Has it ever been truer than today that grandmas come in all shapes and sizes? Like fresh-fallen snowflakes that become a mountain of white, each grandmother is unique. Yes, some of you are still blond, brunette, or redheaded, without a gray hair in sight (thanks, Clairol), and some retain a somewhat girlish figure (thanks, aerobics). More and more of you are still working outside the home, playing tennis, running in marathons, and climbing mountains.

But there are others who have slowed down a bit, acquired a beautiful head of white hair, and spend their time gardening, sewing, and canning. And there are many, many somewhere in between. But, grandmas, while you may not look alike or act alike, there is one thing you all have in common: you are the mothers of your grandchildren's parents. Oh, what a unique position that puts you in.

What childhood secrets are secured in your closets and drawers and under your beds! You are the ones who can look at your grandchild and say, "He acts just like his father" or

"She is the spitting image of her mother." And with this knowledge, you hold the invaluable ability to link the past to the present.

It doesn't matter whether you're forty-four or seventy-four, or whether you play golf on Saturdays or put up peas. It doesn't matter whether you live next door or a thousand miles away. You hold the key, that most important key that unlocks secrets of the past to a wide-eyed child—a child who never thought of his or her parents as children. Secrets that only someone who was there could know. When you think about it, Grandma, you, your husband, and God are the only people in your grandchildren's lives who witnessed the early years of their parents. And just as God, who knows us so well, realizes that deeper knowledge of a person brings understanding and love, you must recognize the power you hold to unite generations with a single story. So tell some stories—remind your children of their past and let your grandchildren know we were all young once.

inspirational message

I want future generations to
remember my *good* advice,
but most of all I want them
to remember my *love.*

• • •

Heather Whitestone

Grandma Shack

"Mom, do I have to take her with me?" Jessica moaned through clenched teeth. "Every time she hears my keys jingle, she picks up her purse! I can't go anywhere without my grandmother!" Jessica had only been seven when her Grandma Shack moved in. At the time of the move, Grandma Shack wasn't feeble by any means. She wasn't sick. She wasn't really that old. There was just no point in her living alone. Nine years had passed, and she still wasn't that feeble or that old. And Jessica was right—she was always ready to go. But a sixteen-year-old with a new car doesn't want her grandmother riding shotgun everywhere she goes.

"Mom, how did she get to be sixty-eight and not get a driver's license?"

Jessica's mom knew this was hard on Jessica. Actually,

it had been hard on the whole family. When her mother-in-law had come to live with them, Jo wanted to make her feel welcome. But she had her six children to consider. Three very active boys and three equally active girls seemed to occupy every available inch of their four-bedroom home. Adding on to their house wasn't an option, so Grandma Shack had to share a room with Jessica, who was the youngest. Now that the older girls were in college, Jessica had moved into their room. Jo knew that over the years, the living arrangement had worked out fine, but she now felt some relief knowing her youngest daughter finally had some privacy.

There was no denying that Grandma Shack wasn't easy to live with. She'd been quick to lay down some ground rules as she rooted out her place in the family nine years earlier. "There will be limited baby-sitting," this strong-willed, tiny Indian woman had said. Jo could still picture her standing there—all four feet, eleven inches tall with stick-straight white hair and hands on her hips. "I raised my children; now you raise yours. And I won't clean up after anyone but myself. I did my share of that also. I don't mind sharing a room, but when my soap operas are on in the afternoon, I like it quiet."

Jo remembered how she joked to her husband, Luke, that Grandma Shack just might make them sign a contract. Once the move was complete, a trunk, a white wicker rocker, a small TV, and twenty shoeboxes with important papers now occupied half of Jessica's pink-and-white ruffled, little-girl bedroom. On more than one occasion, Jo wondered what she had gotten her family into.

"Jessica, just take her with you one more time. I'll talk to your daddy about her. Maybe he can talk to her about letting us know ahead of time when she needs an errand run," Jo pleaded with Jessica.

"Oh, all right," said Jessica. "Maybe I won't see anyone I know!"

"Grandma, I'm ready. Do you still need to pick up some things?" Jessica called down the hallway. There was not even a hint of disrespect in her voice. Jo and Luke had been determined to raise their children to respect their elders, even if they weren't happy with them at the moment.

you have a secret—*share it*

All the children knew Grandma had sacrificed so much to raise her family. Her life had not been easy. Jo often thought that Grandma's face was truly a road map of her life. Each line and wrinkle represented a story in the life of this sometimes aggravating little woman. A woman who struggled to raise six children after leaving an alcoholic, abusive husband. How did she endure so much? Losing a son in a motorcycle accident, sending the four remaining sons off one by one to fight a war, seeing that each child received a proper education—all the time wondering how to put food on the table. *Thank you, God, that my life is easier than Grandma's was,* Jo prayed.

Grandma Shack quickly grabbed her purse and followed her granddaughter out the door. Jessica looked back at her mom and rolled her dark brown eyes. Jo whispered a soft thank-you to her youngest daughter and thought that Jessica really had great patience for a sixteen-year-old. Years of sharing a room with a grandmother probably contributed to that.

As Grandma put her seat belt on, Jessica adjusted the mirror and began backing out of the long driveway. "Where do you need to go today, Grandma?" Jessica asked.

Grandma Shack

"Well, I need a little prune juice, and then I wanted to pick up a card for your daddy's birthday," came the reply. "You know, there was a time when I couldn't even afford a card for your daddy's birthday."

Oh no, thought Jessica, *not another story of how she raised six children with no husband around to help and how she worked in the school cafeteria to support them all.*

Jessica had heard those stories her whole life, and she really did sympathize with her, but did she have to hear them again today? Still she responded politely, "Yes, Grandma, I remember you telling me about those tough years. You really have some great stories. But why don't we talk about today."

Just then a car pulled out in front of Jessica. She slammed on her brakes, but there was no way she could stop soon enough. Jessica could hear the screeching of the tires and then the crunch of metal as the two cars collided.

Then she realized that even though she had hit the car, they were still moving. She reached up and put the car in park and it jolted to a stop. Jessica felt her head lunge forward, and her chin hit hard against the steering wheel.

you have a secret—*share it*

"Jessica, are you OK?" Grandma Shack was yelling. Jessica felt something on her chin and realized it was blood, but she was OK.

"I'm fine, Grandma, what about you?"

"I think so. Just shaken up," she responded.

"Grandma, I can't open my door. I'm getting scared," Jessica cried.

"You're OK. I already hear a police car. Just hang on a minute." Grandma reassured her. Grandma was right. Jessica could hear a siren getting louder and louder.

"Grandma, I'm praying that God will help us get out of this wreck. And when we do, I promise I'll listen to any story you want to tell me about the old days."

The doctors and nurses were so nice at the emergency room. Jessica's teeth had gone through her lip as she hit the steering wheel, and that required several stitches. X-rays were taken and closely reviewed. Jessica and Grandma had pulled some muscles, but no bones were broken.

Friends and family poured into their house all that evening, expressing concern and love. Grandma Shack and Jessica sat side by side, telling their story together. Jessica would begin with what road they were on and how scared she was when she looked up and saw the car pull out in front of them. Grandma would finish the story, telling about Jessica's prayer and promise to listen to her stories. Everyone laughed as Grandma held Jessica's hand and told her she planned to hold her to that promise.

Later that night, after all the visitors left, Grandma and Jessica found that they were more than exhausted. They were also pretty sore. Jessica got her pajamas on and peeked into her old room where Grandma Shack had already climbed into the twin bed she had slept in for the last nine years. She looked over at this old woman who had shared her room for so many years. Funny, what a difference a day makes!

"Grandma, do you mind if I sleep in your room tonight?" Jessica asked.

"Of course not, Jessica. What's on your mind?" Grandma asked.

"I was just thinking how much I appreciate you and the sacrifices you made for your family. And how much you helped me today. Encouraging me to stay calm when I was really scared. There were probably lots of times when you were really scared and there was no one to help you. I just thought you might need me to sleep next to you tonight."

"I think that would be great," Grandma said. "I would love to have someone sleep near me tonight."

"Grandma, now that it's all over and we're OK," Jessica said in a sleepy voice, "I was just thinking how I can't wait to tell my grandchildren the story that we share together. It's a pretty good one, isn't it?"

from *Hugs for Grandma*
by Chrys Howard

chapter **6**

joyful

friend

• • •

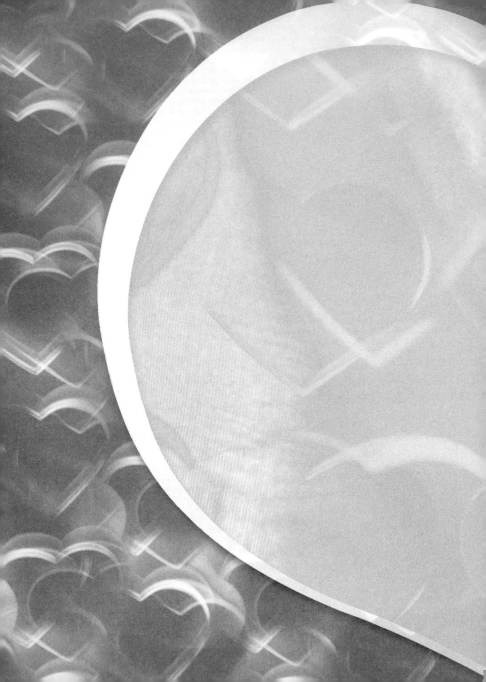

Look for my splashes of joy. Laughter is good medicine—it's a great "shock absorber" for life's unexpected bumps. It helps take the monotony out of everyday life. Don't miss out on the continual feast of a cheerful heart. You'll see that a happy heart bubbles over into a smile. And it's contagious!

Wishing you laughter,
Your God of Joy

—Proverbs 17:22; 15:13–15

F—a friend never fails to be faithful, even when others falter. She won't say, "You're fat" (even if you are), or focus on your flaws. She is the first to point out your finest features. A friend will fortify your fragile frame. She will free you to flourish. A friend will never forsake you.

R—a friend is a rare and ready rock you can run to in the rain. She will rescue you from rushing rivers— regardless. She will revive your heart, refresh your soul, and reassure you of rapid recovery.

I—a friend is not impatient or impolite. She will inquire about your day and include you in her plans. She will identify your most incredible ideas and ingenious innovations. A friend is interesting, inspiring, and indispensable. She is the keeper of your most intimate secrets.

E —a friend is a friend till the end. She is eager to listen and easy to talk with. She's your most energetic encourager. A friend will embrace you even in the midst of your most embarrassing encounters.

N —a friend will not nag (unless it is absolutely necessary). Naturally, she knows your deepest needs and is also nice enough to nudge you when you're neglecting your nest, being too nosy, or contemplating nonsense.

D —a friend is devoted and dependable. Her destiny is to divert you from defeat, and her devices for depression usually involve the delicious. It's a friend's divine duty to drown your disappointments and dispose of your dismay, and many times she does it in a most delightful way!

Laughter is the *language* of the young at heart. And you know what? *You* don't have to be happy to laugh. You become happy *because* you laugh.

• • •

Barbara Johnson

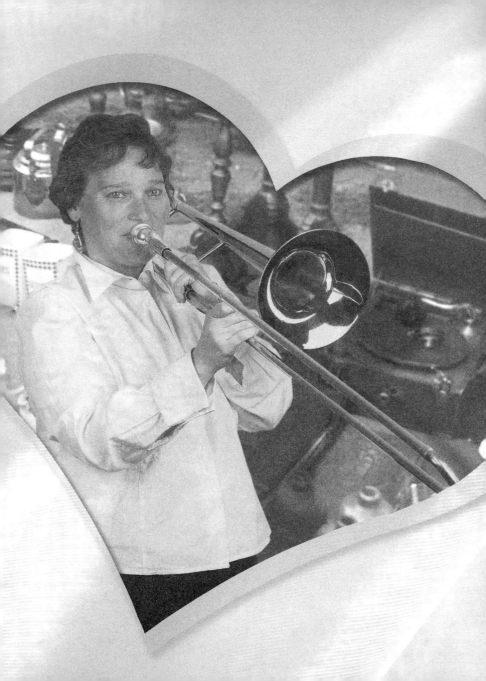

Garage-Sale Escapades

Faced with an empty nest after her three grown boys had flown the coop, Pat sold her spacious 2,500-square-foot Laguna Miguel home and purchased a condo.

Preparing for the big move, Pat realized that over the past seventeen years, she had accumulated a house full of stuff. Since moving into her new condo meant losing 1,000 square feet, Pat had to choose between downsizing and wall-to-wall, floor-to-ceiling boxes. Pat opted for a garage sale.

After countless hours of sorting and tagging a lifetime of memories, the big day arrived. The garage was filled with a collection of bargains—appliances, books, records, knickknacks of every imaginable variety, things her boys no longer wanted, and an assortment of odds and ends.

Huge signs were posted, and a tantalizing ad sure to

attract bargain hunters had been placed in the local newspaper. With the help of her good friend, author and speaker Marilyn Meberg, Pat was armed and ready for the anticipated frenzy of garage-sale addicts. Everything had to go. Pat was eager to sell and prepared to make price-cutting deals to assure that her accumulated loot was hauled away. Pat and Marilyn eagerly took their stations and waited for the customers to pour in.

But Pat had forgotten to take one minor detail into account—the weather. California had been experiencing a heat wave, and this particular Saturday turned out to be the record-breaking day. The thermometer soared to a sweltering 103 degrees. If they had cracked eggs in the miscellaneous pots and pans they were trying to sell, the heat would have fried them.

Pat and Marilyn watched as, one by one, cars began to approach the driveway, slow down, and pause. Occasionally, they could even see noses pressed against the windows as passengers in the air-conditioned cars carefully examined the wares, focusing and pointing at items of interest. But as the two women watched in dismay, each car drove off without actually stopping to ask prices or make a deal. Soon, the "Warning—I brake for garage sales" bumper stickers would drive out of sight.

What a disaster! The sizzling heat was converting die-hard garage-sale junkies into drive-by shoppers. Pat and Marilyn sat in the sweltering heat of the garage, using garage-sale treasures as makeshift fans and guzzling frigid liquids in hopes of avoiding dehydration or sunstroke. Old LP records melted and warped in the sauna-like conditions, and colorful books faded under the intense glare of the sun.

In a valiant effort to divert their attention from the blistering heat, they rummaged through the discarded items looking for access to memory lane. "Remember when you gave in and bought this for the boys?" Marilyn asked as she picked up an old skateboard.

Pat grimaced as she held out an old pair of bell-bottom jeans. "Can you believe these are actually coming back in style?"

"Remember when we were on that health-food fad and you bought this yogurt maker?" Marilyn chuckled.

By early afternoon, only one customer had braved the heat to examine their goods. Dripping with sweat and bored to tears, the two friends were still reminiscing over historic tokens when Pat spotted the old trombone case—a relic from her past. To Marilyn's amazement, Pat picked up the trombone and started blowing.

"Gosh, how long has it been since you played that thing?" Marilyn chaffed in response to the out-of-tune but recognizable song. "I didn't realize you'd ever had lessons."

Out of breath, Pat took a short break to explain that her musical career had started in the second grade. Because her seven-year-old arms had been too short to reach the trombone slide, she used to kick it with her foot. Marilyn laughed as Pat recalled how she had once missed the slide and accidently kicked the music stand off the stage and into the audience during a recital. "It's probably been a good twenty-five years since I've played."

"Hey! Can you play 'When the Saints Go Marching In'?" Marilyn asked. Rising to the challenge, Pat was determined to oblige her friend to the best of her rusty abilities. Although the gritty trombone slide hadn't been oiled in decades, Pat belted out the tune with enthusiasm. Suddenly, the dismal day was transformed into a slaphappy, giddy party as Marilyn began to march around the garage to the beat of the song, arms flailing dramatically as she conducted an imaginary band. Pat energetically joined the march, and the two longtime friends pranced around the garage without a care as to what passersby might think.

Soon, the jocular ruckus began to attract attention. One of Pat's sons emerged from the icy air-conditioned house to see what all the commotion was about, but he quickly buried his face in his hands as he observed his mom and Marilyn laughing and cavorting around the garage with the old trombone. His chagrin only served to energize and encourage their slapstick performance.

Carloads of people actually began to stop to see what all the excitement was about. Some even joined in the escapade with requests of their own. "What about 'Dixie Land'?" "Do you know how to play 'Daisy, Daisy'?" As Pat wholeheartedly tooted away, Marilyn, whose special laughter has earned her a reputation, laughed so raucously that tears were streaming down her face.

Everyone seemed rejuvenated by the jovial mood, in spite of the intense heat. One carload of people turned out to be a group of friends Pat hadn't seen in years, and they enjoyed a surprise reunion.

But despite the crowds their revelry drew, Pat and

Marilyn barely made enough sales to cover the cost of the ad in the paper. One of the few items that did sell was her dad's set of old golf clubs, and she learned too late—just as she sold them for a "song"—that the set was a valuable antique. She ended up donating almost everything to charity, except the sentimental old trombone, which she decided she just couldn't part with. The two weary women were still chuckling when the Salvation Army truck pulled away with a truckload of "priceless treasures." A boring, seemingly wasted day was transformed into a treasured memory by the laughter of friends.

Life is full of unplanned detours, less-than-desirable situations, and downright failures, but we can gain the upper hand if we'll latch on to a friend who can help us hurdle the obstacles of discouragement and defeat. So let your hair down a little and loosen up. Leap into the joyful journey God has tailor-made just for you. As my friend Barbara Johnson says, "The key is learning to look for the splashes of joy in the cesspools of life!"

from *Hugs for Friends*
by LeAnn Weiss

chapter 7

redeemed by
love

· · ·

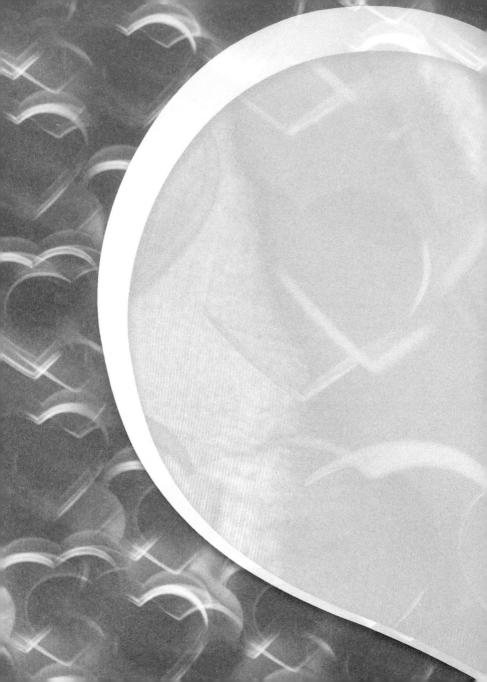

I make you stand firm in Christ. I have anointed you, set My seal of ownership on you, and put My Spirit in your heart as a deposit, guaranteeing what is to come.
I love to do far beyond all you ask or dream through My power, which is working in you—even when you don't realize it.

Planning the best of you,
Your God of Victory

—2 CORINTHIANS 1:21–22; EPHESIANS 3:20

You're a banker and an artist.
You're a sprinter and a florist.
You're an actor. You're a juggler.
You're a queen.

You're a lawyer. You're a manager.
You're a nurse, and you're a counselor.
You do more by noon
Than most have ever seen.

You're a driver and a poet.
A politician (don't you know it!).
You're a botanist, a strategist,
And a judge.

You're a mother and a father.
You're a runner and a tightrope walker.
You're a soldier fighting
In the war on drugs.

You're a diplomat and an acrobat.
You're a farmer. You're a friend.
You tell stories. You mend fences.
You build dreams.

You're an instructor and a trainer,
A communicator and demonstrator.
You're a teacher! You're incredible!
You're supreme!

Mis steffens is the *best* teacher ever. She alwas hellped me *whinever* I needed help. And she also hellped other *peopl* in my class. And when ever we did sumthing rang she *did'nt* talk ferm. She was very nise.

• • •

Daniel, age 8

A Whole New World

"Mrs. Shearin wants you to come to her room. Hurry!" Marcy was out of breath from running when she appeared in my office doorway at the small private school where I was the curriculum coordinator. I quickly followed her through the library and down the hall to Mrs. Shearin's second-grade room. Marcy opened the door, and we stepped into a classroom frozen in awe.

Nine students stood motionless behind their desks, facing the reading table in the back corner. No one moved or looked in our direction as we softly closed the door. A child's voice smoothly intoning sentence after sentence—never missing a word—was the only sound in the room. The other children, still seated at the reading table, were no longer looking at their books but were watching in amazement as their classmate read the text flawlessly. Mrs. Shearin glanced at me with an astonished expression, nodded toward the reader, and turned her attention quickly back to her manual.

The reader was Allen, a child who entered our school after having attended five other schools in the previous two years. His records showed excessive absences, poor academic progress, and frequent discipline problems. His mother had pleaded for his admittance, citing his needs to be in a stable atmosphere and to make friends who were interested in learning. After the mother promised to cooperate with the staff during Allen's adjustment period and made a commitment to his regular attendance, her request was granted.

The first few weeks were difficult. Sheri Shearin was known as a consistent, loving, but firm disciplinarian whose goal was restoring children to productive learning. Allen stretched all of these qualities to the extreme. In the beginning, he would sometimes get so frustrated with schoolwork that he blurted out words that would normally evoke a swift and severe reprimand. But instead, Sheri would call him to her desk, put her arm around him, and say, "Those words are just not tolerated in this school. When you don't know what to do, raise your hand and I'll help you. Now, tell me what you are going to do the next time you feel like that." After he rehearsed the correct procedure, Sheri would assure him that she loved him and believed in his ability to do the right thing. The rest of the class would listen to the softly spoken exchange with rapt attention, knowing that they would never get off that easy. On his third day, he punched a third-grader in the stomach at recess, and his absence for the remainder of the school day was greeted with sighs of relief.

Sheri knew that she could not effect lasting changes in Allen without the understanding and cooperation of his classmates. She also knew that if they could accept him, honor his good points, and love him in spite of his difficult behavior, they would benefit even more than Allen.

Negotiating a fine line between giving Allen the attention he needed and breeding jealousy in the other students, Sheri made time for celebrating the uniqueness and individual successes of each child in the class, and the students responded with new levels of appreciation for one another. She worked hard to orchestrate chances for Allen to be successful in the eyes of the other students. She used Bible stories to teach forgiveness and compassion. She created an atmosphere in which Allen felt accepted—even when he returned from one of his frequent trips to the principal for infractions committed outside the classroom. Students who grumbled at his inattention and slow responses were quietly encouraged to be patient and helpful. Parents who asked about the new boy or volunteered in the room were drawn into the loving-socialization-of-Allen process. Sheri molded her class into a loving community every way she knew how.

Allen had just as much trouble academically as socially. He struggled with simple addition problems, his spelling was atrocious, and understanding the concepts of social studies was almost beyond his grasp. Including Allen in whole-group learning slowed the class down so much that sighs of impatience were regularly heard from the other students. Whenever he was asked to give an answer, everyone had to wait for him to be shown the page the class was on. But nothing seemed to frustrate Allen more than his difficulty with reading. When his turn came in the reading circle, he would stammer and stutter and his face would turn red as he struggled with all his might to make out the words. Of all the things he failed at, it seemed that he wanted to succeed at reading most of all.

And now, Marcy and I stood dumbfounded as we listened to Allen reading flawlessly from his second-grade reader. He was enraptured by the story of a little boy who had a new pair of moccasins. Maybe he felt an affinity for the boy in the story. Maybe his intense desire to read brought all his skills into focus. Maybe the love and acceptance of his teacher and classmates had finally translated into enough self-esteem for him to believe that he could read just as well as his classmates. Whatever the reason, the moment was magic—to Allen, to Mrs. Shearin, to his classmates, and to me.

Allen finished the story and turned to look at Mrs. Shearin, who had tears streaming down her smiling cheeks. She threw her arms around him in a hug of celebration. That's when the applause began.

redeemed by *love*

I'd never seen anything like it before, and I've never seen anything like it since. All Allen's classmates were applauding, and one by one, the remaining seated students rose to their feet to give him a unanimous standing ovation. When his teacher released him, Allen stood beside his chair and bowed deeply—something he had seen a soloist do at a musical performance the previous week. That was when the cheering began.

Allowing the noise to die away naturally, Sheri joined me at the front of the room to watch, as each student congratulated Allen. One of the best readers in the class told him, "I want to read that story again. You made it sound better than when I read it myself."

That day was a watershed for Allen. With his confidence soaring, his reading skills developed rapidly. His self-control and social skills improved steadily, in spite of occasional lapses. He gained a whole year on his skills tests during the second semester alone.

Mrs. Shearin's students experienced firsthand the transforming power of kindness and compassion, and one more child stepped out of confinement and into a whole new world of possibilities.

A Whole New World

Lord, let me be a
Conduit of love and confidence
To children who have known nothing but defeat.
Use me to help each child uncover
The gifts you have placed within.

from *Hugs for Teachers*
by Martha McKee
Messages by Caron Loveless

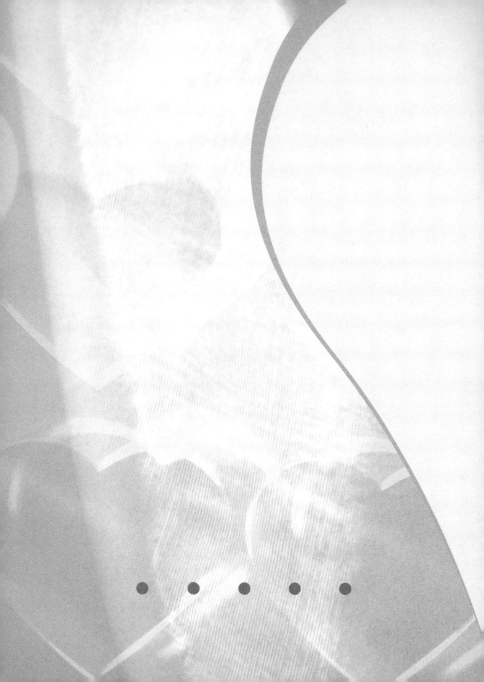

chapter 8

you are
woman

. . .

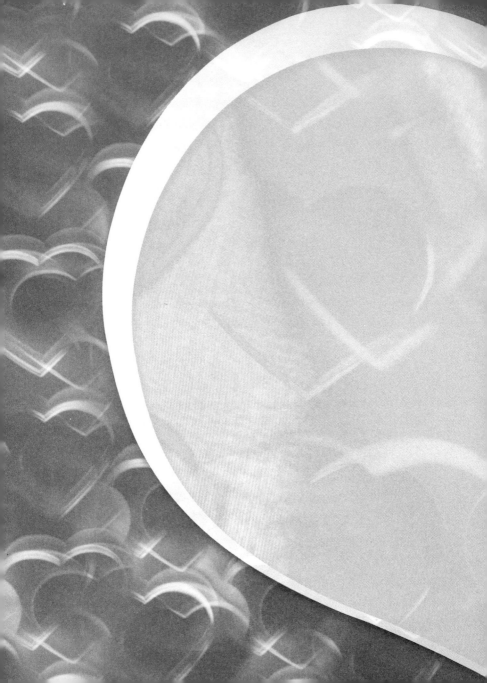

*I have made you rich in every way
so that you can be generous on
every occasion. Your generosity
results in thanksgiving to God.*

Blessing you richly,
Your God of Riches in Glory

—2 Corinthians 9:11

Do you ever get tired of being a woman? Do you sometimes wish you could just be somebody else for a few days?

When you see mountains of laundry, a list of errands as long as your arm, and a stack of paperwork that needed attention yesterday, would you just like to scream and run out the door? "Here, honey, you be the woman this week. Bye!"

And then you would escape to the freedom of no responsibilities—lunch with a friend at that new bistro down the street and a few hours surfing the Net just for fun at www.calm.net. Peace. Quiet. A leisurely stroll along the riverbank, an hour-long bubble bath with a good book and no interruptions, shopping, and a huge helping of death-by-chocolate dessert (without thinking about the calories). No phones. No beepers. No problems to solve. No PMS. No stress. Ahhhhh . . .

Still, think about it. After a few days with no responsibilities, wouldn't you miss the chubby little arms that wrap tightly around your neck? Wouldn't you miss the secret smile that your husband has just for you? Wouldn't you miss your boss's open admiration for the excellent work you do? Wouldn't you miss being "the one in charge" of the community's Fourth of July event? Wouldn't you miss just being you—an amazing, creative, needed, capable, blessed, and loved woman?

God created you as a woman on purpose. It was no accident, no mistake. He specifically made you to fill a role in this life. He endowed you with carefully chosen gifts and abilities to enable you to fill that important role successfully. He depends on you to be who you were created to be.

I recently discovered that the Old Testament Hebrew word for "Holy Spirit" is a feminine word. And I thought, *Of course!* The comforter. The guide. The one who teaches and leads. God created woman after the feminine side of his image. We are the gentle spirit of joy and peace that blesses those around us.

Celebrate! You are God's extended feminine presence in this world. Without you, the world would have an incomplete picture of God. You are woman . . . God's woman.

They talk about a woman's sphere

As though it had a *limit;*

There's not a task to mankind given,

There's not a *blessing* or a woe,

There's not a whispered "yes" or "no,"

There's not a *life,* there's not a birth

That has feather's weight of worth

Without a *woman* in it.

• • •

Speaker's Sourcebook

The Dream

She pulled into town one cool, autumn afternoon, driving slowly down the main street. She stopped at the only traffic light before parking in front of the grocery store. Carolyn bought bread, bologna, cheese, pickles, chips, and a Coke. Then she climbed back into her car and drove to the edge of town, where she noticed a small park in a grove of elm trees. She stopped there to eat her picnic lunch.

As she dumped her trash into the metal barrel, Carolyn caught her breath. There it was! At long last, after her five-year search, she had found it. Tucked into a secluded spot in the woods stood a little cottage—the one she had always imagined as her writing retreat. A dirt path led from the park to the cottage's front gate.

Walking slowly along the path, Carolyn tried to soak

up every detail around the small, deserted building. Fallen elm leaves crunched beneath her feet as she walked reverently through the white picket gate and up the old brick walk to the front porch. She tried the front door, and it opened without resistance. A quick inspection made her heart beat a little faster with anticipation. It was the perfect place for a well-known author to find the anonymity and solitude necessary for writing.

Returning to the front porch, Carolyn sat down in the swing and began to push it gently back and forth, back and forth. Its metal chain squeaked softly in rhythm with her thoughts: *It needs new paint, and the shingles on the roof have to be replaced. The roses need to be pruned, and the lawn has to be mowed. But mostly, it needs someone to live in it, love it, care for it. It's perfect! I wonder why it's empty. Is it for sale?*

A sudden impulse sent Carolyn running back to her car. She drove quickly back into town and found the local real-estate office. When she asked about the little cottage, she learned that it had been repossessed by the bank; its former owners couldn't pay the back taxes. All she had to do was pay the taxes, and it was hers . . . which is exactly what Carolyn did.

The Dream

Handing her the key and deed to her new writing retreat, the real-estate agent told her about a local fix-it man named Henry. He could help her make the needed repairs. Carolyn stopped to talk to him on her way back to the cottage and arranged for him to begin work the next day.

By mid-December all the repairs had been made. The roof no longer leaked, the cottage had a fresh coat of pale-yellow paint and forest-green shutters, the lawn had a manicured look, and Carolyn had added some homey touches inside. It was the perfect haven for writing. Soon she could sit down at her desk overlooking the goldfish pond and begin working on her next novel.

One chilly afternoon as Carolyn swept the leaves off the front porch, she heard a small voice say, "Hello." Looking up, she saw a little red-haired girl swinging on the front gate.

"Well, hello," said Carolyn with a smile. "What's your name?"

"Jenny. What's yours?"

"Carolyn."

"How do you like the house?" the little visitor asked.

"I love it. It's just what I've always wanted."

"We liked it too," said Jenny. "It looks nice with the new paint."

Carolyn stopped sweeping. "Thanks. Did you live here?"

"Yes, until my daddy died. Then we had to move."

"Where do you live now?" Carolyn asked with concern.

"In the shelter downtown."

Carolyn put down her broom and walked out to the gate. "I'm sorry your daddy died. What happened?"

"He was sick for a long time, and he couldn't work. The doctors couldn't make him well. They said he had something called leukemia. He died last year, just before Christmas. Then the bank told Mama that we'd have to move. She cried a lot after that."

"I'm so sorry, Jenny. Say, I've got some lemonade inside. Would you like some?"

"Thanks, but I have to go now. My mom will be worried about me. I have to take care of my baby brother while she cooks dinner at the shelter. Maybe I'll come back sometime."

"Please do," Carolyn said quietly as Jenny walked away,

glancing back at the little cottage wistfully two or three times before she was out of sight.

Suddenly Carolyn's happy little cottage—her dream—seemed sad and lonely. In her mind she could see Jenny and her family playing in the yard. She could imagine the smell of homemade bread baking in the small kitchen. She could hear the sounds of laughter that now seemed to echo eerily in the trees. And she knew what she had to do.

On Christmas Eve, Henry, dressed up in a Santa Claus suit, rang the bell at the downtown shelter. He entered with a happy "Ho Ho Ho!" and started giving presents to all the children. He handed Jenny a special doll with red hair just like hers, and he had a big blue rubber ball for Jenny's baby brother.

The last thing in Santa's sack was an ordinary white envelope. He walked quietly over to Jenny's mother and said, "Sarah, this is for you." Looking quizzically at him, Sarah took the envelope and tore open the sealed flap. When she removed a piece of paper from the envelope, a key fell into her lap. She recognized it immediately. When she looked at the paper, she realized it was the deed to the cottage—with her name on it—marked "Paid in Full."

Tears welled up in her eyes as she pulled out the second piece of paper. The light blue note read, "Please come home. I miss you. Merry Christmas." It was signed, "The Cottage by the Park."

She wandered into their lives, touched them gently, and then selflessly wandered away, never to be seen by them again. She had amazed them with her kindness and generosity. Yet she was no bigger-than-life heroine. She was just an ordinary woman—a woman who gave up her own dream to fulfill someone else's. She was a woman probably very much like you.

from *Hugs for Women*
by Mary Hollingsworth

a day to treasure

family

• • •

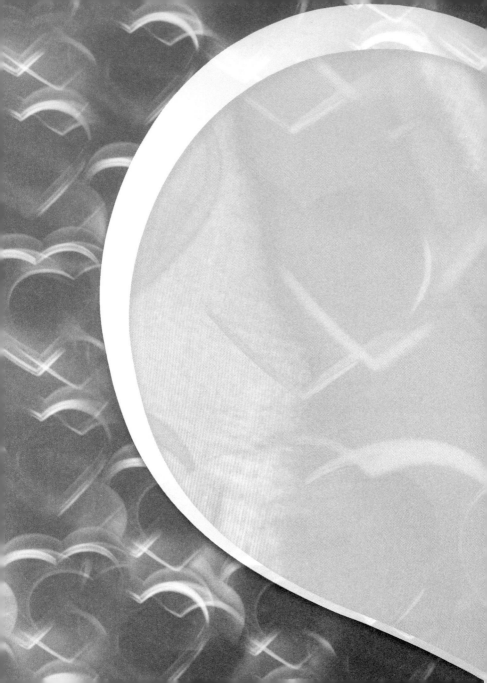

I've given you great treasure in ordinary earthen vessels so you'll be able to see My power and glory within and not be distracted by what's on the outside. I've made My light shine on you to brighten your heart with the knowledge of My glory as revealed in the face of My Son. When you face loneliness, struggles, and hardships, don't fear being crushed or destroyed. Remember, your heart will be where your treasure is. Heavenly treasures are eternal: they can't be stolen or destroyed.

Treasuring you,
Your Heavenly Father

—FROM 2 CORINTHIANS 4:6–9;
MATTHEW 6:20–21

You've heard it said: "You don't know what you've got until it's gone." That holds true especially with those we love. Sometimes life can become so hectic that we forget to really communicate with our families. Sure, we talk and interact about daily necessities, but meaningful, thought-provoking dialogue is often neglected.

When was the last time you stayed up until the wee hours of the morning because you just couldn't stop talking to someone you loved? A simple question about future plans could inspire hours of heart-to-heart conversation. Sometimes it's during those midnight talks that family grows more precious and you come to the realization that you are truly loved.

And you *are* truly loved. Whether

those around you have taken the time to
say it or not, you're admired. Your family may
say it in the little things. Like saving that last
piece of pie for you because it's your favorite. Or
listening to that same old story again because they
know you love to tell it.

Today, find opportunities to spend intimate,
one-on-one time with each member of your family.
Don't wait until you have a large block of time to
share. Steal moments from each day to connect
with them. Take a break from routines and enjoy
special occasions with those you love. Laugh
and make memories. Appreciate the people,
heritage, and traditions that make up your
family. It may just be the best gift you can
give yourself.

Home is not *where*
you live but where they
understand you.

• • •

Christian Morgenstern

Far from Home

Lance Corporal Christopher Davis sat on the steps outside his barracks holding his head in his hands. His camouflage uniform was filthy and soaked with sweat. He clunked the heel of his combat boot on the ground to dislodge several layers of mud. His stomach growled loudly, although he barely felt the hunger pains, having grown accustomed to the sensation.

Christopher had spent the last four months stationed in Cuba, but for the past three weeks he'd been "in the field." With no showers, little food, and not much opportunity for sleep, the field was designed to train soldiers to live in warlike conditions. Right now Christopher was so exhausted, he felt like he'd been through a real battle.

Slowly he pulled himself up and trudged to the room he shared with Bobby, a fellow marine. Emerging from the bathroom, Bobby shook water from his hair. "It's all yours," he said, tucking his towel securely around his waist. "There's no hot water though."

Struggling to pull off a clinging, smelly sock, Christopher shrugged. "Cold water sounds good right now. I've had just about enough of this tropical humidity."

Bobby nodded in agreement. "Yeah, taking a shower hasn't stopped the sweat from dripping down my back. But at least I don't stink!"

"I guess that's all we can ask for in this weather," Christopher answered with a tired laugh as he headed for the bathroom.

As cool water sprayed, dissolving the grime from his face, Christopher tried not to think about being without his family for a whole year. When he had gotten the orders to go to Cuba for twelve months, he dreaded telling his wife and two young sons that they wouldn't be able to accompany him. They'd done their best not to complain too much, but he knew it would be just as hard on them as it was for him. Not only did he miss them terribly, but Christopher also felt guilty about leaving his wife to raise their children alone for such an extended time.

Far from Home

Standing in front of the sink, he examined the beard that had grown in since his last shower almost a month ago. "Well, I might as well shave before my birthday dinner." He knew tonight's meal in the chow hall would be no different than the regular rotation of meat loaf or macaroni and chili. But at least it sounded better than their meals in the field. He'd had his fill of vacuum-packed meals sufficient in calories but less than satisfactory in flavor.

Worn jeans and a white T-shirt felt weightless after weeks of carrying his military gear. Grabbing the small stack of letters that had connected him to home over the past months, Christopher left the room and went to get something to eat.

The mess hall was nearly empty, with only ten minutes left before closing. Rather grateful for the solitude, Christopher carried his tray to an empty corner table. He was glad to find orange gelatin for dessert instead of his least favorite, green gelatin with marshmallows. Bowing his head, Christopher silently blessed his food.

Although he was grateful for many things besides the meal, Christopher couldn't help feeling that this was one of the worst birthdays ever. Taking a large bite of meat

loaf and mashed potatoes, he picked up one of the enve-
lopes he'd brought from his room. It was the most recent
letter from his family.

Distance and time apart had made Christopher treasure
his family more than ever, and reviewing the old letters
seemed to bring them a little closer. Still, reading about
their activities was bittersweet. Christopher couldn't help
but laugh thinking about his seven-year-old son, Michael,
losing a tooth in the middle of Sunday school. He hated
that he'd missed five-year-old Thomas's first T-ball game.
Even though his sweet wife, Susan, insisted that they were
making it "just fine," he knew it had to be hard disciplining
the boys without help and dealing with her own loneliness.

Christopher folded the letter and scooped up a few
more bites of the meat loaf, saving the orange gelatin for
last. Picking up one of the more tattered papers, Christopher saw the picture Michael had drawn. Although it
was supposed to be cheerful, Christopher felt depressed.
Stick figures of his wife and children stood in front of
their house, while his representation was beside a faraway
tree—a painful reminder that the separation was as hard
on his family as it was on him.

Christopher barely tasted his dessert. He headed back to his room feeling guilty for not being around for Susan and the boys, and more lonely than ever. Bobby was just leaving the barracks. "Hey, Chris, you have some mail in the room, and there's a package too."

"Thanks." With a glimmer of hope, Christopher quickened his pace. He could only suppose that the package was from his family.

Rounding the corner, Christopher immediately noticed the large box on his bed. I don't even want to think about how much it cost to mail a package that size. The thought flashed through his mind but was gone in an instant, replaced by his excitement. Sure enough, the label bore Susan's familiar handwriting.

Christopher pulled out his pocket knife and slit the packing tape carefully, so as not to damage any of the items inside. Near the top of the box, under a thin layer of wadded-up newspaper, was a large manila envelope.

Anticipation was at its peak as he tore open the envelope to find a small stack of photographs. He laughed out loud when he saw the images. The first was a picture of his two children wearing birthday hats and standing in front of a birthday cake. Suddenly a small detail caught his eye, and Christopher held the photo closer, not sure he believed what he saw. But it was true. On the cake, in bright red icing letters, were the words "Happy Birthday, Dad!" The second picture showed the boys blowing out candles on the cake.

The third photo quickly became a blur through his tears. It was considerably crooked, obviously taken by one of the boys. As Christopher roughly wiped his cheeks with the back of his hand, Susan looked back at him, smiling as she held a piece of cake out in front of her as if offering it to him. The last snapshot showed the boys each enjoying a rather large piece of his birthday cake. Christopher laughed affectionately, squeezing more tears out of his smiling eyes.

He put the pictures aside and curiously explored the rest of the parcel. Although there was no birthday cake to be found, he was delighted to find a large plastic bag stuffed with his favorite dessert, Rice Krispies Treats. Without a moment's hesitation, he chose the largest he could find and bit down greedily. Christopher closed his eyes to savor the moment. It tasted just like home.

Next he unpacked a dried-macaroni necklace from Thomas and a folded piece of newsprint, most likely a new drawing from Michael. Christopher felt a catch in his heart and held his breath as he started slowly unfolding the paper. What message would he see in this innocent work of art? Don't read too much into it, he told himself as he opened the final fold.

With one glance, Christopher heaved a sigh and grinned broadly, even as his eyes welled up again with tears. There was only one way to interpret this masterpiece, as far as he was concerned. Across the top of the page was written in childlike cursive, "What I want to be when I grow up." Below was a stick figure of Michael, outfitted in what only a trained parental eye would recognize as his brown and green camouflage uniform. It was all the indication Christopher needed to be assured that he was still an important part of his family and could have a positive impact on his children.

With pride, Christopher held the picture to his chest. Even though he was far from home, his family was close at heart. This wasn't the worst birthday after all.

from *Hugs for Your Birthday*
by Stephanie Howard

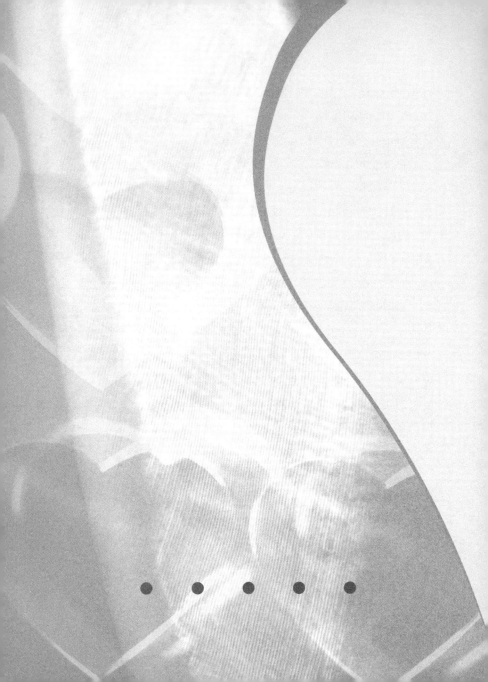

chapter 10

a mother's *home*

• • • •

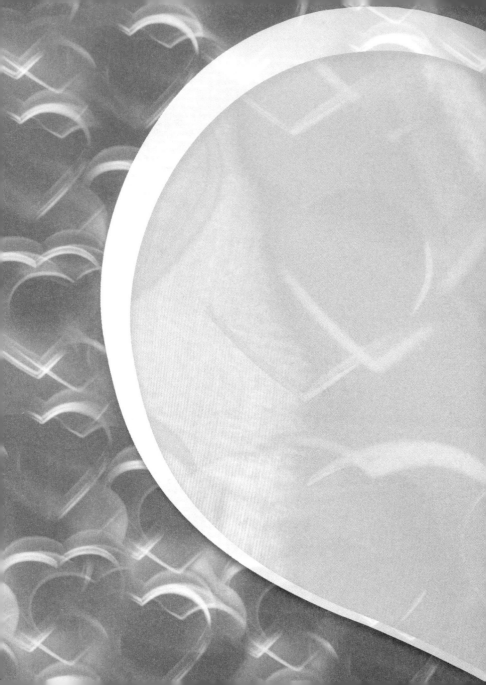

When you wait upon Me, I'll reenergize you and help you to thrive. Build your home with My wisdom and establish it through understanding. Use knowledge to fill its rooms with treasures rare and beautiful. When you hope in Me, you'll never be disappointed.

Renewing you,
Your Creator

—FROM ISAIAH 40:31; PROVERBS 24:3–4;
    ISAIAH 49:23

Mothers are the builders of home. You don't need a special degree or elaborate training. Previous experience is not required. A home is not measured by the number of rooms or the height of the ceilings. It's not defined by how many people live in the house or what kind of neighborhood it's in. It doesn't matter if you're surrounded by extended family or in a new place on your own. In fact, a home is not a physical thing at all.

A home is warmth and hope and support. It's laughter and joy and peace. It's sadness shared and disappointments understood. It's the freedom to grieve and the encouragement to dream. A home is people and relationships. Mostly, a home is love.

But a home does not build itself. It takes effort and determination. It requires purpose and vision. Sometimes it means behaving contrary to the way you feel: getting up when you feel like staying down, moving forward when you're stuck in the past. While building a home takes great effort, it's not beyond your reach. You have within you all that's required to make a true home for those you love.

You have hands that caress and arms that embrace. You have a voice that encourages and lips full of kisses. You have feet that run to help and ears that listen. You have a heart that cares and a love that shares. You are a mother, the builder of your home.

Pleasant memories can give us an immediate cheer-producing mind *switch.*

• • •

Marilyn Meberg

Threads of Love

Ruth's eyes glazed over as she stared out the window above her kitchen sink. No matter how hard she tried, she just couldn't call this little rental house home. It was a house. Nothing more. She had no roots here, no connections. Ruth had left all her connections back home in Southern California where she'd grown up—where all her family still lived.

At first Ruth had been thrilled with Kurt's job offer. A job with a national insurance firm would provide the security they desperately needed for their little family of three. But as the time approached for leaving all that was familiar, Ruth's confidence in their decision dwindled. She'd never lived away from her family before. Who would baby-sit when she and Kurt needed an evening out? Who would make birthdays special?

a mother's *home*

Who would help her teach Crystal all she needed to know? The answer was simple: there would be no one. She was alone.

Of course she had Kurt. And Crystal. She loved being a wife and mom—she really did. But she had grown up part of a big, busy family, and now her family was so small. She was disconnected from all that had made her feel a part—a part of something bigger than herself and her little family.

Ruth finished the dishes, then plopped down on the couch and waited for the bus to bring Crystal home from school. She leaned her head back and closed her eyes. In her mind she was seven years old again and sitting on a footstool at her grandmother's feet. Mama Lou pulled a spool of thread from the top shelf of her sewing chest. The chest stood about twenty-seven inches tall and was made of two beautiful woods—one light and one dark—alternately inlaid for a striped effect. Two drawers held scissors, thimbles, and miscellaneous sewing accessories. A hidden shelf with built-in spool dowels was revealed when the top was opened. Ruth loved the old chest, partly because it was beautiful and partly because the grandfather she barely remembered had made it. But mostly because it reminded her of family.

Mama Lou was threading a needle with a blue thread that perfectly matched the button that had fallen from Ruth's jacket. "Once you have the needle threaded, you tie a knot in the end of the thread, like this." Mama Lou deftly looped the thread around her index finger, twisted it between her thumb and forefinger, and then slid the twisted thread between her thumbnail and finger until it caught in a knot. She held it up for Ruth to see.

"Now you try it," Mama Lou said, handing Ruth a piece of thread. Ruth twisted the thread as she had seen Mama Lou do and pulled it between her fingers, but no knot appeared.

"I can't do it," she pouted. "I never can do anything right!"

"Land sakes alive!" Mama Lou retorted. "Of course you can! You do all sorts of things right. Why, just this morning I saw you helping your mother make banana pancakes, and they were delicious. Here, watch me one more time."

After watching Mama Lou a second time, Ruth picked

up her thread. Sticking her tongue out the corner of her mouth and furrowing her brow in deep concentration, she looped and twisted and slid the thread once again. "I did it, Mama Lou," she exulted. "I did it! I made a knot."

"Of course you did." Mama Lou resumed her sewing matter-of-factly. "You can do most anything you set your mind to."

Ruth beamed with confidence that day long ago. She felt she could indeed do anything. But now, twenty years later, Mama Lou was long gone, and Ruth felt anything but confident. *How am I going to handle Crystal's first crush? I had my mother, my grandmother, and several aunts to help me recover from my first broken heart. And how will Crystal feel with just her dad and me cheering her on at school plays and sporting events? My cheering section was three full rows. I don't like living away from family!*

Just then Ruth heard the door open, and Crystal burst into the room crying. Ruth was kneeling in front of her daughter in seconds. "What is it, honey? What happened?"

Huge tears rolled down Crystal's red cheeks. "Laura and Misty wouldn't let me play with them," she said, her little chest heaving with emotion. "They said I wasn't part of their group! They said they were best friends in kindergarten and first grade, and I just moved here, so they won't let me be their friend."

"Oh, I'm so sorry, honey. I'm sure there are plenty of other girls you can be friends with," Ruth said, feeling not nearly as confident as she tried to sound.

"Why did we have to move away from Grandma and Grandpa? I liked my old school and my old friends! Can we move back, Mommy, can we please?"

I'd do it in a heartbeat if it were up to me, Ruth thought, but aloud she said, "We've only been here a few weeks. It takes time to get used to new people and places. You'll make some friends, honey, you just wait and see."

"Do you really think so, Mommy?" Crystal's crying had slowed, and she looked at Ruth with eyes full of hope and trust.

"I know so." Ruth gathered her daughter in her arms and gave her a reassuring hug. *I've only been away from my family three weeks, and I'm telling my daughter a bald-faced lie. I need my mother!* Ruth fought back her own tears as she comforted her trusting daughter. "It's going to be OK

. . . it's going to be just fine." But Ruth didn't believe a word of it.

The sharp ring of the doorbell made both Ruth and Crystal jump. "Who could that be?" Ruth said as she straightened her hair and gathered her composure. She opened the door to a uniformed delivery person.

"Package for you, ma'am," the young man said. "Please sign here."

Ruth signed for the package and pulled it inside. Tears sprang to her eyes as soon as the door closed. The return address was Cool Valley Road, the California street where her mom and dad lived. It must be another care package from her mother. Last week she had sent a big box with Ruth's two favorite kinds of candy—plain and peanut M&M's—and wheat bread and granola from her favorite health-food store. "I wonder what Grandma has sent us this time?" Ruth said to Crystal. "Why don't you help me open this big box."

Pulling off the many layers of wrapping tape, Ruth finally got the box open. Now she had to dig through several layers of packing paper and peanuts. "Grandma really knows how to keep stuff safe."

Ruth caught her breath, and her tears now flowed unrestrained. She couldn't believe what she saw.

"Why are you crying, Mommy?" Crystal asked. "Don't you like our present?"

"I love it. Sometimes mommies cry when they're happy. Here, you hold the box while I pull out Grandma's surprise."

Slowly, carefully, Ruth pulled out the family heirloom that meant more to her than any other piece of furniture in her mother's house. "It's Mama Lou's sewing chest, Crystal. Grandma has sent me Mama Lou's sewing chest!"

"It's striped—like a zebra." Crystal mused, running her fingers over the inlaid wood. "What's a sewing chest?"

"It's a special place to keep needles and thread and buttons and scissors. See?" Ruth opened one side of the hinged top to reveal several old wooden spools of thread mounted on tiny dowels. "Crystal, look. The spools have writing on them. This one says 'For gold slacks.' Here's another one that says 'For JoAnn's jacket.' JoAnn is your grandma's name."

Ruth picked up a spool of blue thread. "For Ruth's

blue—" Fresh tears filled her eyes. "This is the thread Mama Lou used to sew a button on my jacket when I was a little girl—just about your age." Ruth gently pulled open one of the drawers. Her grandfather's craftsmanship was evident in the chest's tiniest details. Even after all these years, the drawer slid out smoothly, without a hitch. Inside the drawer was a note in her mother's handwriting:

I thought you could use a little reminder of home to help you feel connected with all of us here who love you so much. I'm so proud of you for stepping out to make a home for yourself in a new place. May these threads from the past be a link to your future.

Love,
Mom

"Crystal, bring me your red shirt with the missing button. I'll fix it for you like Mama Lou used to fix my clothes for me."

Crystal quickly retrieved the shirt and then sat on the ottoman by Ruth's chair. She watched intently as Ruth rummaged through the thread looking for just the right color.

Threads of Love

"Once you have the needle threaded, you tie a knot in the end of the thread, like this." Ruth deftly looped the thread around her index finger, twisted it between her thumb and forefinger, and then slid the twisted thread between her thumbnail and finger until it caught in a knot. She held it up for Crystal to see.

"Now you try it." Ruth smiled as Crystal made her first attempt at threading a needle.

For the first time in a long time, Ruth felt peaceful and whole. Distance could not break the connection with her family. They were all irrevocably linked—Mama Lou, her own mother, herself, and now Crystal—held together by threads of love that spanned both space and time.

from *Hugs for Mom*, Book 2
by Philis Boultinghouse

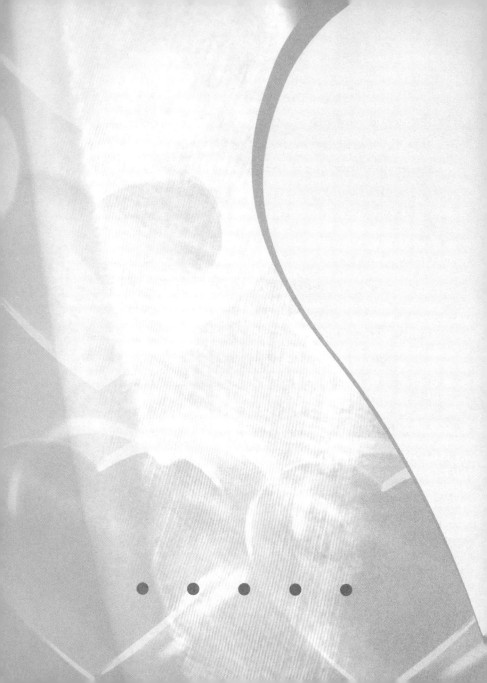

chapter 11

your own hugs
story

• • •

We are *shaped*

and fashioned

by what we *love.*

• • •

*Johann Wolfgang
Von Goethe*

Your Own Hugs Story

Hugs come in all shapes and sizes. They are sometimes a physical hug, but often they come in the form of words spoken, gifts given, or actions taken. Use these pages to write your own "hugs" story, either of a time you were hugged or you were honored to hug someone else. In either case, you were blessed. Enjoy your own "hugs" adventure!

_____

_____

_____

_____

_____

_____

your own hugs *story*

Your Own Hugs Story

your own hugs *story*